ABOUT HABITATS

Mountains

To the One who created mountains.

—*Genesis* 1:1

Published by
PEACHTREE PUBLISHERS
1700 Chattahoochee Avenue
Atlanta, Georgia 30318-2112
www.peachtree-online.com

Text © 2009 by Cathryn P. Sill
Illustrations © 2009 by John C. Sill

Illustrations created in watercolor on archival quality 100% rag watercolor paper.
Text and titles set in Novarese from Adobe.

Printed in Singapore
10 9 8 7 6 5 4 3 2 1
First Edition

Library of Congress Cataloging-in-Publication Data

Sill, Cathryn P., 1953-
  About habitats : mountains / written by Cathryn Sill ; illustrated by
John Sill. -- 1st ed.
     p. cm.
  ISBN 13: 978-1-56145-469-3 / ISBN 10: 1-56145-469-9
  1. Mountains--Juvenile literature. I. Sill, John, ill. II. Title.
  GB512.S55 2009
  577.5'3--dc22
                        2008036743

Mountains

Written by **Cathryn Sill**   Illustrated by **John Sill**

PEACHTREE
ATLANTA

MOUNTAINS FEATURED IN THIS BOOK

ARCTIC OCEAN

Mount McKinley ★

Alaska Range ●

NORTH AMERICA

Olympic Mts. ●

★ Mount Rainier

Teton Range

Cascade Mts. ●

Rocky Mts. ●

Appalachian Mts. ●

Blue Ridge Mts. ●

Mount Mitchell ★

ATLANTIC OCEAN

EUROPE

Alps ●

Dolomites ●

ASIA

Mount Everest

Himalayas ●

PACIFIC OCEAN

PACIFIC OCEAN

SOUTH AMERICA

Andes Mts. ●

AFRICA

Virunga Mts. ●

Mount Kilimanjaro ★

INDIAN OCEAN

AUSTRALIA

ANTARCTICA

PLEASE NOTE: Map and mountain areas are not to scale.
Mountain boundaries are approximate.
● mountains and mountain ranges
★ individual mountains

Mountains

Mountains are places that rise high above the surrounding land.

Most mountains are in groups called ranges.

A few mountains stand alone.

PLATE 3
MOUNT KILIMANJARO

African Elephant

The lower slopes of mountains are warmer than the cold, windy mountaintops.

Some mountains have high peaks that are always covered with ice and snow. Plants and animals are not able to live on the highest mountain peaks.

Some mountains have rounded tops and are covered with trees.

PLATE 6
APPALACHIAN MOUNTAINS

Many kinds of plants and animals are able to live in warmer mountain forests.

PLATE 7
MOUNT MITCHELL
(Blue Ridge Mountains)

Black Bear
Broad-winged Hawk
Eastern Chipmunk
Black-throated Green Warbler
Woodchuck
Flame Azalea
Mountain Laurel

Some mountains are steep and rocky.

Plants and animals living on steep, rocky mountainsides have special ways of surviving.

Plants in high, rocky areas grow close to the ground for protection from strong, cold winds.

PLATE 10
ROCKY MOUNTAINS

Moss Campion
American Pipit

Many animals have special feet that help them move safely on the rocky mountainsides.

Mammals that live high in the mountains
have thick fur coats that keep them warm.

PLATE 12
HIMALAYAS

Snow Leopard

Some animals sleep in dens through the cold winter months.

Others migrate to warmer places farther down the mountain.

Many people live and work on mountains.

Streams and rivers that begin in mountains provide fresh water for people.

Mountains are important places that need to be protected.

Afterword

PLATE 1

Mountains are found on every continent in the world. Movements in the Earth's crust and volcanoes form mountains. Mount McKinley, part of the Alaska Range, is the tallest mountain in North America. Another name for Mount McKinley is Denali, which means "the high one." Caribou live in the Alaska Range as well as in other regions of the far north. The domesticated reindeer of Europe and Asia are descendants of wild Caribou. Unlike other deer, both male and female Caribou have antlers.

PLATE 2

Mountain ranges are made up of peaks, ridges, and valleys. A group of mountain ranges makes up a mountain system. The Teton Range is part of the Rocky Mountain system in North America. Trumpeter Swans nest in wetlands in the Teton Range. They are one of the largest birds in North America.

PLATE 3

Mount Kilimanjaro is the largest freestanding mountain in the world and the tallest mountain in Africa. Mount Kilimanjaro is made up of three inactive volcanoes. African Elephants graze on the flat plains around Mount Kilimanjaro as well as in the forests on the lower slopes of the mountain. Elephants are the largest land animals. They eat grasses, fruit, leaves, bark, and roots.

PLATE 4

Certain types of plants and animals are able to live on the lower, warmer mountain slopes, and different types live near the peaks where the temperature is colder. Deciduous trees that lose their leaves in winter live on the lower mountainsides. Coniferous trees with evergreen needles that shed snow can live farther up the mountain. Black Woodpeckers, the largest woodpeckers in Europe, live in the forests of the Dolomite Mountains in northeastern Italy.

PLATE 5

Life is hard on high mountain peaks. The weather is extremely cold and the winds are harsh. The air at the tops of mountains has less oxygen for animals to breathe and less carbon dioxide for plants to use. The highest mountain in the world is Mount Everest, located in the Himalaya Mountains in Asia.

PLATE 6

Mountain ranges that have rounded tops are older than mountains with sharp rocky peaks. The peaks of older mountains have been slowly worn down over many centuries by wind, water, and ice. The Appalachian Mountains in eastern North America are some of the oldest mountains on Earth.

PLATE 7

The lower slopes of mountains are often covered with thick forests. Since the Blue Ridge Mountains—a part of the Appalachians—are not very tall, they are almost completely forested. The Appalachian Mountains have more different types of trees than any other area in North America. A wide variety of plants and animals lives in this mountain range. Mount Mitchell, the highest mountain in eastern North America, is in the Blue Ridge Mountains.

PLATE 8

The Andes Mountains are the highest mountain ranges outside of Asia. Stretching from one end of South America to the other, they form the longest system of mountain ranges in the world. Andean Condors roost on ledges and nest in shallow caves on the steep cliffs of the Andes. These strong flyers are able to soar in the winds that blow around the mountains.

PLATE 9

Plants and animals living high on mountains have to deal with harsh conditions such as fierce winds and freezing temperatures. The thin soil in this environment makes it harder for plants to get the food they need. Parsley Ferns grow from cracks in rocky areas. Life can be difficult and dangerous for animals on the bare rocks, but many have found ways to safely live there. Wallcreepers live in the Alps in Europe. Their long claws help them cling to cliffs. They use their long, slim bills to get insects and spiders from cracks in the rocks.

PLATE 10

Above the timberline—the highest part of tall mountains—it is too cold and windy for trees to grow. Plants must be short and strong to survive in this environment. Many of these plants form a thick cushion of stems and small leaves that traps heat and protects the plants from the bitter cold. Moss Campion, a wildflower common in high mountains like the Rockies, grows in bare rocky areas. American Pipits nest in the Rocky Mountains.

PLATE 11

The higher slopes of the Rocky Mountains of North America are cold, steep, and rocky. Mountain Goats are able to live there because they have split hooves with rough, rubbery pads to help them grip the steep rocks and slippery ice. Baby Mountain Goats are able to run and jump from rock to rock soon after birth. Mountain Goats eat grasses, lichens, and other low-growing plants on the mountainsides.

PLATE 12

It gets very cold in the high mountains of Central Asia, where fierce winds blow over 100 mph (160 kph). Snow Leopards use their long, thick tails like blankets, wrapping them around their bodies and faces for protection from cold winds. Their tails also help them balance as they chase prey across steep slopes. Some people hunt Snow Leopards for their beautiful fur or for their bones and body parts, which they think make good medicines. Snow Leopards are endangered and it is illegal to hunt them in most places.

PLATE 13

Many animals in the high mountains cannot find food in winter because the plants they eat have died back or are covered with snow. Olympic Marmots live in family groups that hibernate in the same burrow from September to May. Sharing the burrow may help them stay warm. Olympic Marmots are found only in the Olympic Mountains in the northwestern United States. They eat grasses and other green plants.

PLATE 14

Animals that live on mountains can protect themselves from the worst weather by moving from place to place to find food or shelter. When the snows begin in autumn, Gray-crowned Rosy-Finches migrate to the lowlands where it is warmer. In spring, they move back up the mountains where they nest in cracks along rock cliffs. Gray-crowned Rosy-Finches nest on high mountains in western North America, including Mount Rainier, a dormant (inactive) volcano in the Cascade Range.

PLATE 15

About 10 percent of the world's population lives in mountain areas. Many people who live on mountains grow crops for food. Farmers cut small fields called terraces into the sides of the steep mountains to keep the soil from washing away. Other people who live on mountains raise animals such as llamas or yaks to provide them with milk, meat, and wool. Some mine valuable minerals found in the mountains or cut trees growing on the mountains to sell as lumber.

PLATE 16

Mountains are sometimes called nature's water towers. The water in mountain streams and rivers comes from rain or melting snow and ice. Most of the major rivers in the world begin in mountains. Half of the people on Earth depend on water that comes from mountains. Cullasaja Falls is located on the Cullasaja River in the southern Appalachians. The Cullasaja joins other streams and rivers that flow into the Tennessee River. The Tennessee River is an important source of water for many people in the southeastern United States.

PLATE 17

Many mountain environments are fragile because of the harsh conditions there. Human activities such as mining, farming, development, and tourism can also cause lasting damage on mountains by destroying the only places where certain plants and animals can live. People that work, live, or vacation on mountains need to protect these fragile habitats. Mountain Gorillas, found only in the Virunga Mountains in east-central Africa, are very rare. They are seriously threatened by destruction of the forests where they live and by illegal hunting.

GLOSSARY

BIOME—an area such as a wetland or mountain that shares the same types of plants and animals

ECOSYSTEM—a community of living things and their environment

HABITAT—the place where animals and plants live (A mountain can support many types of habitats, including deciduous hardwood forests, coniferous forests, alpine meadows, and tundra.)

Crust—the rocky surface of the Earth

Den—a place where wild animals rest or sleep

Peak—the top part of a mountain

Prey—animals that are hunted and eaten by other animals

Ridge—a long, narrow mountain range or hilltop

Slope—rising or falling ground

Valley—low land between mountains or hills

Volcano—an opening in Earth's crust where lava (melted rock), gases, and ashes are forced out

BIBLIOGRAPHY

BOOKS

AMERICA'S MOUNTAINS: GUIDE TO PLANTS AND ANIMALS by Marianne D. Wallace (Fulcrum Publishing)

ANIMALS OF THE HIGH MOUNTAINS by Judith E. Rinard (National Geographic Society)

MOUNTAIN ANIMALS by Francine Galko (Heinemann Library)

PROTECTING MOUNTAIN HABITATS by Robert Snedden (Gareth Stevens Publishing)

WEBSITES

http://42explore.com/mountain.htm

http://www.mountain.org/education/

http://library.thinkquest.org/11353/mountain.htm

http://www.scionline.org/index.php/category:Alpine_tundra

Also by the Sills:

ABOUT THE SILLS

Cathryn Sill, a former elementary school teacher, is the author of the acclaimed ABOUT... series. With her husband John and her brother-in-law Ben Sill, she coauthored the popular bird-guide parodies, A FIELD GUIDE TO LITTLE-KNOWN AND SELDOM-SEEN BIRDS OF NORTH AMERICA, ANOTHER FIELD GUIDE TO LITTLE-KNOWN AND SELDOM-SEEN BIRDS OF NORTH AMERICA, and BEYOND BIRDWATCHING.

John Sill is a prize-winning and widely published wildlife artist who illustrated the ABOUT... series and coauthored the FIELD GUIDES and BEYOND BIRDWATCHING. A native of North Carolina, he holds a B.S. in Wildlife Biology from North Carolina State University.

The Sills live in Franklin, North Carolina.

Books in the ABOUT... and ABOUT HABITATS series

ISBN 978-1-56145-028-2 HC
ISBN 978-1-56145-147-0 PB

ISBN 978-1-56145-141-8 HC
ISBN 978-1-56145-174-6 PB

ISBN 978-1-56145-183-8 HC
ISBN 978-1-56145-233-0 PB

ISBN 978-1-56145-207-1 HC
ISBN 978-1-56145-232-3 PB

ISBN 978-1-56145-234-7 HC
ISBN 978-1-56145-312-2 PB

ISBN 978-1-56145-256-9 HC
ISBN 978-1-56145-335-1 PB

ISBN 978-1-56145-038-1 HC
ISBN 978-1-56145-364-1 PB

ISBN 978-1-56145-301-6 HC
ISBN 978-1-56145-405-1 PB

ISBN 978-1-56145-331-3 HC
ISBN 978-1-56145-406-8 PB

ISBN 978-1-56145-358-0 HC
ISBN 978-1-56145-407-5 PB

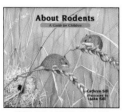

ISBN 978-1-56145-454-9 HC

ISBN 978-1-56145-390-0 HC

ISBN 978-1-56145-432-7 HC

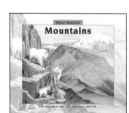

ISBN 978-1-56145-469-3 HC